A Picture Book of
Patrick Henry

David A. Adler

illustrated by John & Alexandra Wallner

Holiday House/New York

Other books in David A. Adler's *Picture Book Biography* series

For Jacob Neumark
D.A.A.

For our friend, Brian Klinger
Love,
Alex and John

Text copyright © 1995 by David A. Adler
Illustrations copyright © 1995 by John and Alexandra Wallner
ALL RIGHTS RESERVED
Printed in the United States of America

Library of Congress Cataloging-in-Publication Data
Adler, David A.
A picture book of Patrick Henry / David A. Adler ; illustrated by
John & Alexandra Wallner. — 1st ed.
p.   cm.
ISBN 0-8234-1187-7
1. Henry, Patrick, 1736–1799—Juvenile literature.
2. Legislators—United States—Biography—Juvenile literature.
3. United States. Continental Congress—Biography—Juvenile
literature.   4. United States—Politics and government—1775–1783
—Juvenile literature.   5. Virginia—Politics and
government—1775–1783—Juvenile literature.   [1. Henry, Patrick,
1736–1799.   2. Legislators.]   I. Wallner, John C., ill.
II. Wallner, Alexandra, ill.   III. Title.
E302.6.H5A63   1995   94-43849   CIP   AC
973.3'092—dc20
[B]

ISBN 0-8234-1678-X (pbk.)

Patrick Henry was born on May 29, 1736 at Studley Farm, a tobacco plantation in Hanover County, Virginia. Virginia then was one of the thirteen American colonies ruled by England.

Patrick's parents were Sarah and John Henry. John Henry was a farmer, judge, surveyor, and soldier. Patrick was the second of their eleven children.

Patrick studied at a nearby one-room school house and at home with his father. His favorite subjects were mathematics and history. But Patrick loved guns and hunting more than books. He liked fishing, too, and could sit for hours by the edge of a creek, waiting for fish to bite.

When Patrick Henry was eleven a new minister came to town, the Reverend Samuel Davies. He was a powerful speaker. He would speak softly, then shout, and then lower his voice again. Patrick Henry said later that Reverend Davies was the greatest speaker he had ever heard. Patrick Henry would be a great speaker, too.

At age fifteen, Patrick worked as a clerk in a country store. The next year John Henry bought some tea, coffee, spices, and other goods and set up his sons Patrick and William in a store of their own.

The wealthy farmers didn't buy from the Henry brothers, but poor farmers did because the Henrys sold on credit, which is the promise to pay later. By the end of their first year in business, Patrick and William had lots of credit slips but very little money. They also had very little left to sell. They had to close the store.

About the time Patrick had worked in his store, he began courting a neighbor, Sarah Shelton. She was said to be "dear and sweet" and pretty, too. They married in October 1754 in the parlor of the Shelton home. Patrick was eighteen and Sarah was only sixteen. The young couple moved onto three hundred acres of land Sarah's father had given them as a wedding gift. He also gave them six African-American slaves.

For a few years Patrick struggled with his slaves to work the farm. But in 1757, a fire destroyed his house and most of his belongings. A short while later he gave up farming. He moved with his family into a tavern owned by Sarah's father. It was near the Hanover Court House.

Patrick sold a few of his slaves, bought some goods, and opened another store. The store was busy, but not always with customers. Often people stopped by just to talk. And some days, when Patrick Henry should have been minding his store, he was in the Hanover Court House instead.

Patrick Henry listened to all the legal talk and arguments. It interested him. When his store failed, Patrick Henry decided to become a lawyer.

He studied law and in 1760 passed his exams. Within his first three years as a lawyer Patrick Henry handled more than one thousand cases. At last he was a success.

It was said that when Patrick Henry spoke in court, "There was lightning in his eyes" and in his voice "a peculiar charm, a magic."

On December 1, 1763, Patrick Henry tried his first big case, the Parson's Cause. The parsons objected to a law passed by the people of Virginia. The king of England supported the parsons and rejected the law.

Patrick Henry defended the people. He said the king had no right to veto a law passed by the people. He called the king a tyrant.

"The gentleman has spoken treason," accused the parsons' lawyer.

Perhaps he had. But Patrick Henry won his case.

Patrick Henry was famous now. He was made a member of the Virginia House of Burgesses, where laws were passed.

The French and Indian War, in which England and France fought for American territory, ended in 1763. In March 1765, to help pay for the war, the British Parliament passed the Stamp Act, a tax on printed matter sold in the colonies. In May, in the House of Burgesses, Patrick Henry spoke out against the tax.

"Treason! Treason!" people called out after hearing him speak. "If this be treason," Patrick Henry answered, "make the most of it."

The House of Burgesses objected to the Stamp Act. Other colonies did, too.

In 1766 the British Parliament dropped the Stamp Act. But in 1767 it passed the Townshend Acts—new taxes for the American colonists to pay. The colonists protested and in 1770 Parliament ended every tax but the one on tea.

On December 16, 1773, to protest the tea tax, colonists disguised themselves as Native Americans and boarded English ships anchored in Boston Harbor. They broke up 342 chests of British tea and threw them into the water.

The thirteen American colonies were headed toward war with England.

Meanwhile, Patrick Henry was having trouble at home. He and and his wife Sarah had six children. The youngest, Edward, was born in 1771. With the birth of Edward, Sarah became ill. The family doctor later wrote that Sarah had "lost her reason." Her arms were tied and she was locked in a room so she wouldn't harm herself or others. The doctor also wrote that during Sarah's illness Patrick's "soul was bowed down and bleeding under the heaviest of sorrows and personal distress." Sarah Henry died in 1775.

Patrick was still active in politics. In 1774 he was elected to represent Virginia at the First Continental Congress in Philadelphia. Delegates from twelve colonies met there to find a way to deal with King George of England and Parliament.

Patrick Henry called for the delegates to think of themselves as a united people. "The distinctions between Virginians, Pennsylvanians, New Yorkers, and New Englanders are no more. I am not a Virginian, but an American."

In March 1775 Patrick Henry spoke before the Virginia Convention. "Gentlemen may cry peace, peace," he said, "but there is no peace . . . Is life so dear, or peace so sweet, as to be purchased at the price of chains and slavery? Forbid it, Almighty God! I know not what course others may take but as for me, give me liberty or give me death!"

These strong words came just one month before the first shots were fired in the American Revolution.

Patrick Henry was a delegate to the Second Continental Congress, too. But on July 4, 1776, when it approved the Declaration of Independence declaring the people of America free of English rule, Patrick Henry was in Virginia. A new state government had been formed and he was elected Virginia's first governor. He was re-elected governor in 1777, 1778, 1784, and 1785.

In 1777, during Patrick's second term as governor, he married a much younger woman, Dorothea Dandridge. She was a cousin of Martha Washington, the wife of America's first president. Patrick and Dorothea had eleven children together.

The fighting of the Revolution continued until October 1781 when the Americans won an important battle at Yorktown, Virginia. Two years later, on September 3, 1783, the Americans and British made peace. They signed the Treaty of Paris.

Patrick Henry spoke out against the new Constitution of the United States. He thought it was "dangerous . . . horribly frightful. . . Your president may easily become king." And the colonies had just fought a revolution to be free of kings.

Patrick Henry lost his argument. But his fears and the concerns of others led to the passage of the Bill of Rights, ten amendments to the Constitution protecting people's rights.

President George Washington admired Patrick Henry and asked him to be minister to Spain or France, Secretary of State, or Chief Justice of the Supreme Court. Patrick Henry didn't take any of these jobs. In 1796 Patrick Henry was elected governor of Virginia and refused to serve. He was tired of public service and he needed to earn money to support his big family.

In 1799 Patrick Henry finally agreed to return to public life. He ran for a seat in the Virginia state legislature and won. But he was already ill with cancer. He died three months later, on June 6, 1799 at the age of sixty-three.

Patrick Henry was called the "Noble Patriot." He is one of our nation's Founding Fathers. A Virginia newspaper, in reporting his death, wrote, "Mourn Virginia, mourn! Your Henry is gone! . . . Farewell, first-rate patriot, farewell!"

AUTHOR'S NOTE

In an 1817 biography by William Wirt, Patrick Henry is described as "coarse . . . his dress slovenly . . . no persuasion could bring him to read or work. On the contrary, he ran wild in the forest." While this description has been repeated in many later biographies, historians have found it to be mostly fiction.

Patrick Henry called slavery "an abominable practice . . . destructive to liberty" and "evil." And yet, he had many slaves, more than sixty at the time of his death. He explained that he kept slaves because it would be just too difficult "living here without them."

IMPORTANT DATES

1736	Born in Hanover County, Virginia on May 29.
1754	Married Sarah Shelton.
1760	Became a lawyer.
1763	Tried his first big case, the "Parson's Cause."
1764	Elected to the Virginia House of Burgesses.
1765	Spoke out against Stamp Act.
1774–5	Delegate to the Continental Congress.
1775	Gave "Give me liberty or give me death" speech on March 23. First wife Sarah died.
1776	First elected governor of Virginia. He was re-elected in 1777, 1778, 1784, and 1785.
1777	Married Dorothea Dandridge on October 9.
1799	Died in Charlotte County, Virginia on June 6.